7 Steps for EMPOWERING YOUTH
Self-Awareness ★ Developing GRIT... *and* a Growth Mindset

James Louis Cantoni, Sr.

Publisher: Realizing Dreams
                    Glastonbury, CT 06033 ★ USA

Published in: Glastonbury, CT
Typography by: Realizing Dreams
First printed as Teamwork and FamilyPlay - Empowering youth through self-discovery. Pilot printing April 2013 Second printing April 2014 Third Printing May 2014 Fourth Printing June 2015 as 7 Steps for EMPOWERING YOUTH: Self-Awareness Developing GRIT... and a Growth Mindset
Cantoni, James Louis, Sr, 1960-
7 Steps for Empowering Youth - Self-Awareness Developing GRIT *and* a Growth Mindset
Cover images and book illustration by Realizing Dreams

1) Conduct of life-Quotations, maxims, goal setting, etc 2) Happiness-Quotations, maxims, etc.

I. Title. 7 Steps for Empowering Youth - Developing GRIT and a Growth Mindset

ISBN - 978-0-9903128-3-3   (v.1, 2, 3 & 4, paperback)

Printed in the United States of America

For my wife Jackie,

You are my sunshine.

– Jim

For my two boys,

Nathan, I cherish your smiles, giggles and hugs.
Jimmy, <u>I Love You Two</u>.

– Dad

For my mom and dad,

Mom, you are everything to me.
Dad, I miss you.

– Jimmy

"Let us think of education as the means of developing our greatest abilities, because in each of us there is a private hope and dream which, fulfilled, can be translated into benefit for everyone and greater strength for our nation."

– John F. Kennedy

"DO THE BEST IN MY LIFE"

The Theory of Our Purpose in Life™

"**I**nspire **P**otential in **O**urselves so that we can **I**nspire **P**otential in **O**thers.

Engage, equip and empower youth to realize their dreams, achieve greater life outcomes, and create a legacy greater than ourselves."

– Jim Cantoni
Author, Founder and Practitioner

"If your actions inspire others to dream more, learn more, do more, and become more, you are a leader."

– *John Quincy Adams (1767 – 1848)*
Sixth President of the United States (1825–1829)

7 Steps for EMPOWERING YOUTH

Synchronizing Generations. *Transforming Lives.*™

Have you ever heard an adult say, "I wish I was your age and knew what I know now?" Unfortunately, we all have. I need your help to change that. Pronounced "E to the second power", E^2™ is a formula created to put youth and adults on the same page.

The BIG Questions are:

> *Which "E" do **youth** have more of?*
>
> *Which "E" do **adults** have more of?*

We all know that youth have more energy in our youthfulness and adults have more experience with our age. It is when we arrive at that special place - *with everyone on the same page* - and synchronize the "energy and experience" of generations, that youth learn from the life lessons and mistakes of adults. Ultimately, we will learn the "easier way" in life so we can transform and improve the lives of others.

In a nutshell, synchronizing generations is what this self-discovery "LifeBook" is all about. It is through this insight into our youth's interests, hopes, dreams, goals, fears, worries and aspirations, that we can synchronize generations. The purpose is to engage, equip and empower our youth to reach their full potential, realize their dreams and achieve greater life outcomes.

Be in the 3...

83 14 3%

Learn by doing what research shows to be a predictor of success in school, work, life and play.

7 Steps for EMPOWERING YOUTH makes it easier for you to be in the top 3% of the most successful people in life. They are self-aware, set **Goals**, work smart, then hard and focus their efforts to achieve their goals in life. They are "**Gritty**" and have a **Growth Mindset**. Most importantly, they believe that they can realize their dreams. *Now, you're on your way too!*

Realizing Dreams In Teams™
Connecting Schools, Families and Communities to Improve Youth Outcomes

REALIZING
★ Dreams ★
Engage. Equip. Empower.™

Me and the 9 Self's
For Emotional Intelligence

Self-Propelled
with Self-Management
for Self-Sufficiency
and Self-Actualization

Self-Discovery

Realizing Dreams in Teams™
Student Centered
Teachers/Parents/Mentors Involved

Self-Awareness

Self-Worth

Self-Control

Self-Efficacy

Grit, Goal Setting & Growth Mindset

First, here is one of The BIG Questions for you! What did Thomas Edison, Henry Ford, Eleanor Roosevelt, Steven Jobs, Rosa Parks, Elizabeth Cady Stanton, Nelson Mandela, Dr. Martin Luther King, Jr. and other greats in life all have in common?

I believe these greats were all empowered with self-awareness, Grit, Goal Setting and a Growth Mindset - all predictors of success. In doing so, these truly remarkable people were able to improve not only their lives, but most of all, they developed the passion to improve the lives of countless others.

"What exactly is self-awareness?" Socrates a famous philosopher who was born around 470 BC, perhaps said it best with, *"Know thyself."* To help increase your self-awareness of your interests, hopes, dreams, goals, worries, fears and aspirations in life, this "lifebook" is all about your future and giving you a voice and choice in your life - *today.* Hopefully, you will feel empowered giving your "MBA" - My Big Answer to some of The BIG Questions in your life. I thank Robby Kasper, who at only 16 years old, came up with the idea for My Big Answer and is helping further inspire us all as Socrates teaches us to "Know thyself".

Got Grit? According to Dr. Angela Duckworth, a distinguished UPENN Researcher whose work is based on proven predictors of success that help youth reach their potential, *"Self-control is the short-term ability to resist temptations and, say, get your schoolwork done; grit is what* *takes you the distance. Grit is passion and perseverance for very long-term goals. Grit is having stamina. Grit is sticking with your future, day in, day out, not just for the week, not just for the month, but for years, and working really hard to make that future a reality. Grit is living life like it's a marathon, not a sprint."*

Do you think you have a Growth Mindset? Simply stated, a growth mindset is believing that you can improve. It's like what Henry Ford thought, whether you think you can or think you can't, you're right. Dr. Carol Dweck, a renowned Stanford researcher found "every time they [students] push out of their comfort zone to learn something new and difficult, the neurons in their brain can form new, stronger connections, and over time they can get smarter." Dr. Dweck's research also shows that teaching people to have a growth mindset and to focus on effort rather than on intelligence or talent, helps transform them into high achievers in school and in life. It turns out that this focus on our effort increases our grit!

In her closing line on Ted Talks, Dr. Angela Duckworth challenges adults with, ***"We need to be gritty about getting our kids grittier."*** Hopefully, all of this will further illuminate the power of self-awareness, grit, goal setting and a growth mindset like in the Edison's, Einstein's, Roosevelt's, Dr. King's, other greats in the world, and now you. At 54 years young, one of my dreams is for you to realize at your young age to think critically and plan your future today. Then, one day, you will wake up happy unlike many adults who often realize too late that more than half of their life has passed away. These adults wish they knew what they know now at your age. My other dream is to also inspire you to focus your efforts, persevere and get out of your comfort zone. When you challenge yourself to reach higher, set and achieve your GETTING SMARTR™ goals as the *7 Steps for EMPOWERING YOUTH* shows you, you can realize your dreams. ***Chances are, with these predictors of success, you will change the world too!***

A Note to Readers:

Students... *Jump right in and start with the 7 Steps on page 1!*

Parents and Guardians... First, all the activities in *7 Steps for EMPOWERING YOUTH* can be facilitated by you or your child. The activities will help you spark the social and emotional conversations that you want to have with your family. If you play along, you will find out what makes you a strong and valuable part of your child's life. Feel free to flip through the pages or start from the beginning. Find your favorite trait along with your child's. Compare–find what is the same or what is different. What can you as a family build upon to bring a new depth to your relationships? This is something everyone wants and needs to help their children reach their full potential.

Teachers, Mentors, Counselors and Youth Development Professionals... As valuable partners in the lives of children everywhere, you, as a leader, coach and professional have a rare opportunity to bring a child's life to "life". Through experiencing the self-discovery activities included in this "Lifebook" along with your class, group or PTA/ PTO Parent/Family Engagement team, you will see your students in a new light. You will discover what is important to those you want to guide to success. You will gain insight that will help students create strategies for dealing with challenging situations. Students will begin to shine as they discover their passion and realize their self-worth. *You will also be empowering your school's Student Success Plans!*

Students will see themselves in a new way– they will create a true focus on their hopes and dreams. The discussions and collaborative activities will build bridges between generations and create strong bonds among peers. Students can even teach other students and will find it very empowering! You will make a difference and change a life. Enjoy the self-discovery, the learning, and the creating of visions of the future as you put those you care about on the path to success.

– Claudia Danna, Retired Director of Curriculum and Instruction, Bolton Public Schools

Table of Contents

Clearly SEE Your Path
to a Successful Future

Learn-by-Doing with "Predictors of Success" for up to 10x the Success in YOUR life!

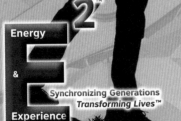

Energy
&
Experience

E²™

Synchronizing Generations
Transforming Lives™

REALIZING
★ *Dreams* ★
Engage. Equip. Empower.™

www.RealizingDreams.us

7 Steps for EMPOWERING YOUTH

7 You are self-aware, have GRIT and a growth mindset. You can now reach your full potential.

6 Select and write in your "My Faves" what inspired you most. Set a goal to complete the other pages.

5 Reflect, then select your Top 5 Character Strengths for mindful self-awareness.

4 Go to Page 110 "My Declaration to Realize My Dreams"
Clearly see your path to a successful future. Set your GETTING SMARTR™ Goals. Create your life action plan. Work smart, then hard, have self-control and <u>focus</u> your efforts on your next steps so your dreams come to life.

3 Give Your "MBA", My Big Answer, to The BIG Questions in your life.
Did you select yes? Go to Step 4. If not, go to The BIG Question that inspires you!

2 Flip through your lifebook, select your favorite Character Trait.
Reflect on the meaning of the quotes. Which is your fave? Write your reason why.

1 Complete your Dream Tag™ on the inside front cover.

Realize your dreams...

Character

"People grow through experience if they meet life honestly and courageously. This is how character is built."

— Eleanor Roosevelt (1884 - 1962)

"Character is forged in the smallest of struggles. Then, when the big challenges come, we're ready."

— Waiter Rant, Waiter Rant weblog, 12.30.05

The BIG Question:
You have learned many things in life. What is one of the most useful?

Of these two quotes about Character, my favorite is by:

_____

My reason why:

_____

_____

_____

My Big Answer - **One of the most useful things I learned in life is:**

_____

_____

_____

My reason why:

_____

_____

_____

I would like to also learn: _____

Initial if yes: _____ Date: ____/____/_____ *If you selected yes, go to the pages starting on 110.*

When you complete it, come back and put the date you accomplished it here: ____/____/_____

Communication

"Communications without intelligence is noise;
Intelligence without communications is irrelevant."
— *General Alfred Gray, USMC*

"Of all of our inventions for mass communication,
pictures still speak the most universally understood
language."
— *Walt Disney*

The BIG Question:
**Super Heroes have many different powers. If you could
choose one power for yourself, what would it be and why?**

Of these two quotes about Communication, my favorite is by:

_____

My reason why is:

_____

_____

_____

My Big Answer - **The Super Hero power I would like to have is:**

_____

_____

_____

My reason why:

_____

_____

_____

I will use my imagination of having this superpower but in real life, I will act like a superhero by doing something good for someone.

Initial if yes: _____ Date: ____/____/_____ _If you selected yes, go to the pages starting on 110._

When you complete it, come back and put the date you accomplished it here: ____/____/_____

Creativity

"Creativity is the power to connect the seemingly unconnected."

— *William Plomer (1903 - 1973)*
South African Author, Novelist, Poet and Literary Editor

"The problem is never how to get new, innovative thoughts into your mind, but how to get old ones out. Every mind is a building filled with archaic furniture. Clean out a corner of your mind and creativity will instantly fill it."

— *Dee Hock, Founder and Former CEO of VISA*

The BIG Question:

If you could be an eyewitness to any big event in history, what would it be and why?

Of these two quotes about Creativity, my favorite is by:

_____

My reason why is:

_____

_____

_____

My Big Answer - I would like to be an eyewitness to this event in history:

_____

_____

_____

My reason why:

_____

_____

_____

I will read about this event in history to learn more about it.

Initial if yes: _____ Date: ____/____/_____ *If you selected yes, go to the pages starting on 110.*

When you complete it, come back and put the date you accomplished it here: ____/____/_____

Appreciating Diversity

"Diversity is the one true thing we all have in common. Celebrate it every day."

— *Anonymous*

"If we cannot end now our differences, at least we can help make the world safe for diversity."

— *John F. Kennedy (1917 - 1963)*

The BIG Question:

What is one thing you are learning to do well?

Of these two quotes about Diversity, my favorite is by:

_____

My reason why is:

_____

_____

_____

My Big Answer - **One thing I am learning to do well is:**

_____

_____

_____

My reason why:

_____

_____

_____

I would like to also learn: _____

Initial if yes: _____ **Date:** ____/____/_____ *If you selected yes, go to the pages starting on 110.*

When you complete it, come back and put the date you accomplished it here: ____/____/_____

Helpfulness

"One day a small boy tried to lift a heavy stone, but couldn't budge it. His father, watching, finally said, "Are you sure you're using all your strength?"
"Yes, I am!" the boy cried.
"No, you're not," said the father. "You haven't asked me to help you."
— *Unknown*

"All for one, one for all!"
— *The Three Musketeers*

The BIG Question:

If you could speak another language, which would you choose and what would you use it for?

Of these two quotes about Helpfulness, my favorite is by:

_____

My reason why is:

_____

_____

_____

My Big Answer - **The language I would choose to speak is:**

_____

_____

_____

My reason why:

_____

_____

_____

I will learn this language and use it to communicate with others for the greater good.

Initial if yes: _____ Date: ____/____/_____ *If you selected yes, go to the pages starting on 110.*

When you complete it, come back and put the date you accomplished it here: ____/____/_____

HONESTY

"Where is there dignity unless there is honesty?"
— *Cicero, Philosopher*

"My motto —
first honesty, then industry, then concentration."
— *Andrew Carnegie (1835 -1919)*
Founder of Carnegie Corporation

The BIG Question:

**If you could travel back in time or
into the future, where would you go and why?**

Of these two quotes about Honesty, my favorite is by:

_____

My reason why is:

_____

_____

_____

My Big Answer - I would like to travel back in time or in the future to:

_____

_____

My reason why:

_____

_____

_____

I will learn more about this time (if history) or I will write about what this time in the future will be like.

Initial if yes: _____ **Date:** ____/____/_____ *If you selected yes, go to the pages starting on 110.*

When you complete it, come back and put the date you accomplished it here: ____/____/_____

Leadership

"Leadership is communicating to people their worth and potential so clearly that they come to see it in themselves."

— Stephen Covey
Author of 7 Habits of Highly Effective People

"Give leadership ... Get dedication."
— GivaGeta™

The BIG Question: Who is one person you admire or look up to as a role model? What influence have they had in your life?

Of these two quotes about Leadership, my favorite is by:

_____

My reason why is:

_____

_____

_____

My Big Answer - **The person I admire or look up to as a role model in my life is:**

_____

_____

_____

The influence they had is:

_____

_____

_____

I will send them a heartfelt thank you and share their inspiration with others.

Initial if yes: _____ Date: ____/____/_____ *If you selected yes, go to the pages starting on 110.*

When you complete it, come back and put the date you accomplished it here: ____/____/_____

Give a positive attitude ...
Get a Positive Attitude
— *GivaGeta™*

"The greatest discovery of my generation is that a human being can alter their life by altering their attitude."
— *William James (1842-1910)*
American Psychologist

"I am determined to be cheerful and happy in whatever situation I may be; for I have learned from experience that our happiness or misery depends upon our dispositions and not upon our circumstances."
— *Martha Washington (1732-1802)*
The first First Lady of the United States

The BIG Question: What would you do if you knew you could not fail?

Of these two quotes about a Positive Attitude, my favorite is by:

_____

My reason why is:

_____

_____

_____

My Big Answer - **If I could not fail, I would:**

_____

_____

My reason why:

_____

_____

_____

I will try to do this until I succeed and will seek help of others as needed.

Initial if yes: _____ **Date:** _____/_____/_____ *If you selected yes, go to the pages starting on 110.*

When you complete it, come back and put the date you accomplished it here: _____/_____/_____

Respect

"If you want to be respected by others, the great thing is to respect yourself. Only by that, only by self-respect will you compel others to respect you."

— *Fyodor Dostoevsky (1821 - 1881)*
Author

"Give respect ... Get respect."
— *GivaGeta™*

The BIG Question:

What is something you have always dreamed about doing?

Of these two quotes about Respect, my favorite is by:

_____

My reason why is:

_____

_____

_____

My Big Answer - I have always dreamed about doing:

_____

_____

_____

My reason why:

_____

_____

_____

I will realize this dream!

Initial if yes: _____ Date: ____/____/_____ *If you selected yes, go to the pages starting on 110.*

When you complete it, come back and put the date you accomplished it here: ____/____/_____

Responsibility

"I believe that every right implies a responsibility; every opportunity an obligation; every possession a duty."

— J.D. Rockefeller (1839-1937)
American Industrialist and Philanthropist

"The more freedom we enjoy, the greater the responsibility we bear toward others as well as ourselves."

— Oscar Arias Sanchez
President of Costa Rica (2006-), 1987 Nobel Peace Prize

The BIG Question:

Who is (or was) one of your friends in elementary school and what do you like about him or her?

Of these two quotes about Responsibility, my favorite is by:

_____

My reason why is:

_____

_____

_____

My Big Answer - **One of my friends in elementary school is/was:**

_____

_____

_____

I like them because:

_____

_____

_____

I will be sure to tell them this in my own special way.

Initial if yes: _____ **Date:** ____/____/_____ _If you selected yes, go to the pages starting on 110._

When you complete it, come back and put the date you accomplished it here: ____/____/_____

Teamwork

"To succeed as a team is to hold all of the members accountable for their expertise."
— *Mitchell Caplan, Former CEO of E* Trade Group Inc.*

"Give teamwork ... Get results."
— *GivaGeta™*

The BIG Question:
If you could excel at any sport or activity, what would it be and why?

Of these two quotes about Teamwork, my favorite is by:

_____

My reason why is:

_____

_____

_____

My Big Answer - **The sport I would like to excel at is:**

_____

_____

My reason why:

_____

_____

_____

I will apply myself to the best of my abilities and practice regularly so I can excel at this. I will also read and learn from other greats who have done this before.

Initial if yes: _____ **Date:** ____/____/_____ *If you selected yes, go to the pages starting on 110.*

When you complete it, come back and put the date you accomplished it here: ____/____/_____

Trust yourself.
Create the kind of self that you
will be happy to live with all your life.
Make the most of yourself by fanning the tiny,
inner sparks of possibility into flames of achievement.

– Golda Meir (1898-1978)
Former Prime Minister of Israel

"I know God will not give me anything
I can't handle. I just wish that He didn't
trust me so much."

– Mother Teresa (1910 - 1997)

The BIG Question:

**What is one of the funniest outfits or costumes
you or someone you know ever wore?**

Of these two quotes about Trust, my favorite is by:

_____

My reason why is:

_____

_____

_____

My Big Answer - **The funniest thing I or someone else wore was:**

_____

_____

_____

The reason I thought it was funny is:

_____

_____

_____

I will find a way to top this!

Initial if yes: _____ Date: ____/____/_____ *If you selected yes, go to the pages starting on 110.*

When you complete it, come back and put the date you accomplished it here: ____/____/_____

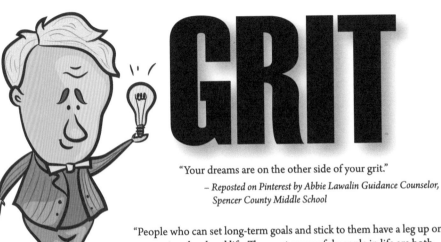

GRIT

"Your dreams are on the other side of your grit."

– Reposted on Pinterest by Abbie Lawalin Guidance Counselor,
Spencer County Middle School

"People who can set long-term goals and stick to them have a leg up on success in school and life. The most successful people in life are both talented and gritty in whatever they've chosen to do."

– Deborah Perkins-Gough, Senior Editor
Association for Supervision and Curriculum Development

Thomas Edison

The BIG Question:
What is one thing that you are most worried about and why?

Of these two quotes about GRIT, my favorite is by:

_____

My reason why is:

_____

_____

_____

My Big Answer - **The one thing I am worried about most is:**

_____

_____

_____

My reason why is:

_____

_____

_____

I will be "GRITTY" and create a plan to overcome my worries so I can be successful in life, realize my dreams and share with others how I overcame this!

Initial if yes: _____ Date: ____/____/_____ *If you selected yes, go to the pages starting on 110.*

When you complete it, come back and put the date you accomplished it here: ____/____/_____

Character

"Character is what you have left when you've lost everything you can lose."

— *Evan Esar (1899 - 1995)*
American Humorist and Author

"Personality can open doors, but only character can keep them open."

— *Elmer G. Leterman*
Author and Founder of the Leterman-Gortz Corporation

The BIG Question:
Who in the world would you like to spend an entire day with?

Of these two quotes about Character, my favorite is by:

_____

My reason why is:

_____

_____

_____

My Big Answer - I would like to spend an entire day with:

_____

_____

_____

My reason why:

_____

_____

_____

Here I set a goal to do this and will learn how to make this happen.

Initial if yes: _____ Date: ____/____/_____ *If you selected yes, go to the pages starting on 110.*

When you complete it, come back and put the date you accomplished it here: ____/____/_____

Communication

Communication
Communication

"If you don't have something nice to say,
don't say anything at all."
— To Thumper from Bambi

"The most important thing in communication is
to hear what isn't being said."
— Peter Drucker (1909 - 2005)
Legendary Management Consultant

The BIG Question:
If you could have any vehicle on the
planet, what would it be and why?

Of these two quotes about Communication, my favorite is by:

_____

My reason why is:

_____

_____

_____

My Big Answer - **The vehicle on the planet I would like to have is:**

_____

_____

_____

My reason why:

_____

_____

_____

Here I set a goal to get this. I will write the manufacturers and tell them of my goal.

Initial if yes: _____ Date: ____/____/_____ *If you selected yes, go to the pages starting on 110.*

When you complete it, come back and put the date you accomplished it here: ____/____/_____

Creativity

"Creativity is allowing yourself to make mistakes. Art is knowing which ones to keep."
— *Scott Adams, Creator of the Dilbert comic strip*

"Creativity is not the finding of a thing, but the making something out of it after it is found."
— *James Russell Lowell (1819 - 1891)*
Author and Co-founder of the American Dialect Society

The BIG Question:

What is one of your favorite things to do on a rainy day and why?

Of these two quotes about Creativity, my favorite is by:

_____

My reason why is:

_____

_____

_____

My Big Answer - **My favorite thing to do on a rainy day is:**

_____

_____

_____

My reason why:

_____

_____

_____

I will do this again and share it with my loved ones and friends.

Initial if yes: _____ Date: ____/____/_____ *If you selected yes, go to the pages starting on 110.*

When you complete it, come back and put the date you accomplished it here: ____/____/_____

Appreciating Diversity

"At the bottom everyone knows well enough that they are a unique human being, only once on this earth; and by no extraordinary chance will such a marvelously picturesque piece of diversity in unity as they are, ever be put together a second time."

> — *Friedrich Nietzsche (1844 - 1900)*
> *German Philosopher and Classical Philologist*

"What we have to do ... is to find a way to celebrate our diversity and debate our differences without fracturing our communities."

> — *Hillary Clinton, 67th United States Secretary of State,*
> *Senator and Former First Lady*

The BIG Question:

What is something that you were told to do and you didn't do, but later wish you had done?

Of these two quotes about Diversity, my favorite is by:

_____

My reason why is:

_____

_____

_____

My Big Answer - I was told to do:

_____

_____

_____

My reason why I wish I had done this is:

_____

_____

_____

Next time I will do it the way I was told and be sure to pass this life lesson along!

Initial if yes: _____ Date: ____/____/_____ *If you selected yes, go to the pages starting on 110.*

When you complete it, come back and put the date you accomplished it here: ____/____/_____

Helpfulness

"Be helpful. What counts a great deal in life is what we do for others."

— *Anonymous*

"Do not let what you cannot do interfere with what you can do."

— *John Wooden*
  Coach and Member of the
  Basketball Hall of Fame

The BIG Question:

What do you think is your purpose in life?

Of these two quotes about Helpfulness, my favorite is by:

_____

My reason why is:

_____

_____

_____

My Big Answer **- My purpose in life is:**_____

_____

_____

_____

My reason why I believe it is:

_____

_____

_____

I use my efforts, gifts of focus, perseverance and self-control to make my purpose in life a reality.

Initial if yes: _____ Date: ____/____/_____ *If you selected yes, go to the pages starting on 110.*

When you complete it, come back and put the date you accomplished it here: ____/____/_____

HONESTY

"Honesty is the best policy."
— *Mark Twain (1835 - 1910)*

"No legacy is so rich as honesty."
— *William Shakespeare (1564 - 1616)*

The BIG Question:

If you could live (or experience) one day over again, what would it be and why?

Of these two quotes about Honesty, my favorite is by:

_____

My reason why is:

_____

_____

_____

My Big Answer - What I would like to live over or experience again is:

_____

_____

_____

My reason why:

_____

_____

_____

I will do this or something similar again and even make it better!

Initial if yes: _____ Date: ____/____/_____ *If you selected yes, go to the pages starting on 110.*

When you complete it, come back and put the date you accomplished it here: ____/____/_____

Leadership

"A leader knows the way, goes the way and shows the way."

— *Stephen Covey*
Author of 7 Habits of Highly Effective People

"Management is doing things right; leadership is doing the right things."

— *Peter Drucker (1909 - 2005)*
Father of "Modern Management"

The BIG Question: What is your favorite pair of shoes and why do you like them?

Of these two quotes about Leadership, my favorite is by:

_____

My reason why is:

_____

_____

_____

My Big Answer - **My favorite pair of shoes and why I like them is:**

_____

_____

My reason why:

_____

_____

_____

Someday, I will get someone less fortunate than me a pair of shoes like these too!

Initial if yes: _____ Date: ____/____/_____ *If you selected yes, go to the pages starting on 110.*

When you complete it, come back and put the date you accomplished it here: ____/____/_____

Give a positive attitude ...
Get a Positive Attitude
— GivaGeta™

"A strong positive mental attitude will create more miracles than any wonder drug."

— Patricia Neal, Actress

"Ability is what you're capable of doing. Motivation determines what you do. Attitude determines how well you do it."

— Lou Holtz
Former Legendary College & NFL Head Coach

The BIG Question: What is the most unusual food combination you like to eat?

Of these two quotes about a Positive Attitude, my favorite is by:

_____

My reason why is:

_____

_____

_____

My Big Answer - **The most unusual food combination I like to eat - or would like to eat - is:**

_____

_____

_____

My reason why:

_____

_____

_____

I will learn how to cook healthy foods and snacks. Then, I will serve them to my friends!

Initial if yes: _____ Date: ____/____/_____ *If you selected yes, go to the pages starting on 110.*

When you complete it, come back and put the date you accomplished it here: ____/____/_____

Respect

"Self-respect is the cornerstone of all virtue."
— *John Herschel (1792 - 1871)*
English Mathematician, Astronomer and Chemist

"For to be free is not merely to cast off one's chains, but to live in a way that respects and enhances the freedom of others."
— *Nelson Mandela*

The BIG Question:

What would you do if you were invisible for a day?

Of these two quotes about Respect, my favorite is by:

_____

My reason why is:

_____

_____

_____

My Big Answer - **If I was invisible for a day, I would:**

_____

_____

My reason why:

_____

_____

_____

I may not be able to be invisible, however I will do something positive for someone and not seek anything in return for it, as if I was invisible to them.

Initial if yes: _____ Date: ____/____/_____ _If you selected yes, go to the pages starting on 110._

When you complete it, come back and put the date you accomplished it here: ____/____/_____

Responsibility

"You cannot escape the responsibility of tomorrow by evading it today."
— *Abraham Lincoln (1809 - 1865)*

"Few things help an individual more than to place responsibility upon him, and to let him know that you trust him."
— *Booker T. Washington (1856 - 1915)*
Educator, Orator and Author

The BIG Question:

If you were the leader of your country (ie. President of the United States), what would you change?

Of these two quotes about Responsibility, my favorite is by:

_____

My reason why is:

_____

_____

_____

My Big Answer - **If I was the leader of my country, I would change:**

_____

_____

_____

My reason why:

_____

_____

_____

In positive ways, I will write the leader and advocate (show support) for this change.

Initial if yes: _____ Date: ____/____/_____ *If you selected yes, go to the pages starting on 110.*

When you complete it, come back and put the date you accomplished it here: ____/____/_____

Team**work**

"Here's my advice for everyday –
a little teamwork and a lot of teamplay."

— *Jim Cain, Author*

"Individual commitment to a group effort –
that is what makes a team work, a company
work, a society work, a civilization work."

— *Vince Lombardi (1913 -1970)*
Legendary NFL Head Coach

The BIG Question:

**If you could eat lunch with any three
people, any time, anywhere, who would
you choose and why?**

Of these two quotes about Teamwork, my favorite is by:

_____

My reason why is:

_____
_____
_____

My Big Answer - **I would like to eat lunch with the following people at this place:**

_____
_____
_____

My reason why:

_____
_____
_____

Here I set a goal to do this! I will take positive actions to make this happen.

Initial if yes: _____ Date: ____/____/_____ _If you selected yes, go to the pages starting on 110._

When you complete it, come back and put the date you accomplished it here: ____/____/_____

"As soon as you trust yourself,
you will know how to live."

— *Johann Wolfgang von Goethe (1749 - 1832)*
Author of Faust

"I trust that everything happens for a reason,
even when we're not wise enough to see it."

— *Oprah Winfrey*

The BIG Question: **If you could have a million of anything to give away (other than money), what would you choose? And who would you give it to?**

Of these two quotes about Trust, my favorite is by:

_____

My reason why is:

_____

_____

_____

My Big Answer - I would like to have a million of:

_____

_____

_____

The reason I would give it to _____ is:

_____

_____

_____

Someday, I will do this and help others in need.

Initial if yes: _____ Date: ____/____/_____ *If you selected yes, go to the pages starting on 110.*

When you complete it, come back and put the date you accomplished it here: ____/____/_____

GRIT

Thomas Edison

"It doesn't matter where you are from or what your skills are, but if you have GRIT you can be successful in life."

– Abbie Lawalin
  Guidance Counselor – South Spencer Middle School

"One thing we've found is that children who have more of a growth mindset tend to be grittier. The correlation isn't perfect, but this suggests to me that one of the things that make you gritty is having a growth mindset. The attitude 'I can get better if I try harder' should help make you a tenacious, determined, hard-working person."

– Angela Lee Duckworth
  Author, Psychologist - University of Pennsylvania

The BIG Question: **In which ways are you "gritty"?**

Of these two quotes about GRIT, my favorite is by:

_____

My reason why is:

_____

_____

_____

My Big Answer - I am "gritty" in these ways:

_____

_____

_____

My reason why I am gritty is:

_____

_____

_____

I will use my grit and growth mindset to realize my dreams in life.

Initial if yes: _____ Date: ____/____/_____ *If you selected yes, go to the pages starting on 110.*

When you complete it, come back and put the date you accomplished it here: ____/____/_____

Character

"Our character is what we do
when we think no one is looking."
— *H. Jackson Brown, Author*

"Nearly all men can stand adversity,
but if you want to test a man's character,
give him power."
— *Abraham Lincoln (1809 - 1865)*

The BIG Question:
Think back to when you were very young.
What is one of the first great memories you have?

Of these two quotes about Character, my favorite is by:

_____

My reason why is:

_____

_____

_____

My Big Answer - **One of the first things I can remember is:**

_____

_____

_____

My reason why:

_____

_____

_____

I will make a positive impact and help others create great memories.

Initial if yes: _____ Date: ____/____/_____ *If you selected yes, go to the pages starting on 110.*

When you complete it, come back and put the date you accomplished it here: ____/____/_____

Communication

"The more elaborate our means of communication, the less we communicate."
— *Joseph Priestley, Discoverer of Oxygen (1733 - 1804)*

"This 'telephone' has too many shortcomings to be seriously considered as a means of communication. The device is inherently of no value to us."
— *Western Union internal memo, 1876*

The BIG Question:

What is one of your favorite TV shows?

Of these two quotes about Communication, my favorite is by:

_____

My reason why is:

_____

_____

_____

My Big Answer - **One of my favorite TV shows is:**

_____

_____

_____

My reason why:

_____

_____

_____

I will learn more about the broadcasting and/or social media industry.

Initial if yes: _____ Date: ____/____/_____ *If you selected yes, go to the pages starting on 110.*

When you complete it, come back and put the date you accomplished it here: ____/____/_____

Creativity

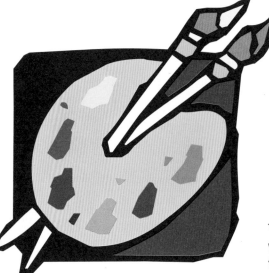

"Creativity can solve almost any problem. The creative act, the defeat of habit by originality, overcomes everything."

> — *George Lois*
> *Former Art Director, Esquire Magazine*

"Creativity is piercing the mundane to find the marvelous."

> — *Bill Moyers*
> *White House Press Secretary (1965-1967)*

The BIG Question:

What is (or was) one of your favorite childhood songs?

Of these two quotes about Creativity, my favorite is by:

_____

My reason why is:

_____

_____

_____

My Big Answer - **My favorite childhood song is/was:**

_____

_____

_____

My reason why:

_____

_____

_____

I will buy this song (or create a new one) and sing it to someone who I think would like it too!

Initial if yes: _____ Date: ____/____/_____ *If you selected yes, go to the pages starting on 110.*

When you complete it, come back and put the date you accomplished it here: ____/____/_____

Appreciating Diversity

"Darkness cannot drive out darkness: only light can do that. Hate cannot drive out hate: only love can do that."
— *Dr. Martin Luther King, Jr. (1929-1968)*

"Recognize yourself in he and she who are not like you and me"
— *Carlos Fuentes, Author (1928-2012)*

The BIG Question:

If you could have an extra hour each day, how would you like to spend it?

Of these two quotes about Diversity, my favorite is by:

_____

My reason why is:

_____

_____

_____

My Big Answer - **If I had an extra hour each day, I would spend it:**

_____

_____

_____

My reason why is:

_____

_____

_____

This is important to me and my life, I will find a way to accomplish this.

Initial if yes: _____ Date: _____/_____/_____ _If you selected yes, go to the pages starting on 110._

When you complete it, come back and put the date you accomplished it here: _____/_____/_____

Helpfulness

"Make service your first priority, not success and success will follow."
— *Author Unknown*

"The aim (of education) must be the training of independently acting and thinking individuals who, however, can see in the service to the community their highest life achievement."
— *Albert Einstein (1879 - 1955)*

The BIG Question:

What is something helpful that someone has told you and how did it help?

Of these two quotes about Helpfulness, my favorite is by:

_____

My reason why is:

_____

_____

_____

My Big Answer - **Someone once told me:**

_____

_____

_____

It helped because:

_____

_____

_____

I will share this helpful advice!

Initial if yes: _____ Date: ____/____/_____ *If you selected yes, go to the pages starting on 110.*

When you complete it, come back and put the date you accomplished it here: ____/____/_____

HONESTY

"If our actions stem from honesty, kindness, caring, and vision, then no matter what the result of our efforts, we have added something of value to our souls and to the world."

— Joan Borysenko, Ph.D.
Author of *Pocketful of Miracles*

"Honesty is the first chapter of the book of wisdom."

— Thomas Jefferson (1743 - 1826)

The BIG Question:

Of all the positive words people use to describe you, which one do you like the most?

Of these two quotes about Honesty, my favorite is by:

_____

My reason why is:

_____

_____

_____

My Big Answer - **The positive word I like the most when people describe me is:**

_____

_____

_____

My reason why:

_____

_____

_____

I will tell others what positive things I like about them!

Initial if yes: _____ **Date:** ____/____/_____ *If you selected yes, go to the pages starting on 110.*

When you complete it, come back and put the date you accomplished it here: ____/____/_____

Leadership

"Good leadership consists in showing average people how to do the work of superior people."

— *John D. Rockefeller (1839 - 1937)*
American Industrialist and Philanthropist

"I start with the premise that the function of leadership is to produce more leaders, not more followers."

— *Ralph Nader*

The BIG Question: Which teacher was one of your favorites and why?

Of these two quotes about Leadership, my favorite is by:

_____

My reason why is:

_____

_____

_____

My Big Answer - **My favorite teacher is/was:**

_____

_____

_____

My reason why:

_____

_____

_____

I will write them a note and tell the teacher this! Or if the teacher is in Heaven, I will say a prayer for them showing my appreciation for helping me reach my potential.

Initial if yes: _____ **Date:** ____/____/_____ *If you selected yes, go to the pages starting on 110.*

When you complete it, come back and put the date you accomplished it here: ____/____/_____

Give a positive attitude ...
Get a Positive Attitude
— GivaGeta™

"Ultimately, contentment is more a shift in attitude than a change in circumstances."

— Linda Dillow
Author of Calm My Anxious Heart

"Weakness of attitude becomes weakness of character."

— Albert Einstein (1879 - 1955)

The BIG Question: What is something that you can do really well?

Of these two quotes about a Positive Attitude, my favorite is by:

_____

My reason why is:

_____

_____

_____

My Big Answer - **The one thing I can do really well is:**

_____

_____

_____

My reason why:

_____

_____

_____

I will keep getting better at this and share my learning to help others!

Initial if yes: _____ Date: ____/____/_____ _If you selected yes, go to the pages starting on 110._

When you complete it, come back and put the date you accomplished it here: ____/____/_____

Respect

"Never esteem anything as of advantage to you that will make you break your word or lose your self-respect."

— *Marcus Aurelius Antoninus (121 AD - 180 AD), Meditations*

"Among the individuals, as well as among nations, respecting other people's rights leads to peace."

— *Benito Juarez Garcia (1806 - 1872) Former President of Mexico*

The BIG Question:

If you could have any one talent (ie. singing, drawing, playing an instrument), what would it be?

Of these two quotes about Respect, my favorite is by:

_____

My reason why is:

_____

_____

_____

My Big Answer - The one talent I would like is:

_____

_____

_____

My reason why:

_____

_____

_____

Here I set a goal and I will focus my efforts to acquire (obtain) this talent!

Initial if yes: _____ Date: ____/____/_____ *If you selected yes, go to the pages starting on 110.*

When you complete it, come back and put the date you accomplished it here: ____/____/_____

Responsibility

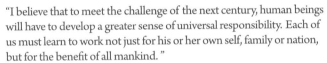

"I believe that to meet the challenge of the next century, human beings will have to develop a greater sense of universal responsibility. Each of us must learn to work not just for his or her own self, family or nation, but for the benefit of all mankind. "

— *His Holiness the Dalai Lama*

"The price of greatness is responsibility."

— *Winston Churchill (1874 - 1965)*

The BIG Question:
What is one of your favorite things to do on a sunny day and why?

Of these two quotes about Responsibility, my favorite is by:

_____

My reason why is:

_____

_____

_____

My Big Answer - **One of my favorite things to do on a sunny day is:**

_____

_____

_____

My reason why:

_____

_____

_____

I will do this again, and perhaps even share this experience with a special friend!

Initial if yes: _____ Date: ____/____/_____ *If you selected yes, go to the pages starting on 110.*

When you complete it, come back and put the date you accomplished it here: ____/____/_____

Team**work**

"When you're part of a team, you stand up for your teammates. Your loyalty is to them. You protect them through good and bad, because they'd do the same for you."

> — *Yogi Berra*
> *Catcher/Manager, Baseball Hall of Fame*

"Talent wins games, but teamwork and intelligence wins championships."

> — *Michael Jordan*

The BIG Question:

What is something you've done in your life that you are proud of?

Of these two quotes about Teamwork, my favorite is by:

_____

My reason why is:

_____

_____

_____

My Big Answer - **Something that I have done and am proud of is:**

_____

_____

_____

My reason why:

_____

_____

_____

I will do this again or do something else that will make me and others proud.

Initial if yes: _____ **Date:** ____/____/_____ *If you selected yes, go to the pages starting on 110.*

When you complete it, come back and put the date you accomplished it here: ____/____/_____

"One of the most important ways to manifest integrity is to be loyal to those who are not present. In doing so, we build the trust of those who are present."

— *Stephen Covey*
  Author of 7 Habits of Highly Effective People

"When I'm trusting and being myself ... everything in my life reflects this by falling into place easily, often miraculously."

— *Shakti Gawain, Author and Environmentalist*

The BIG Question: **Name three things that you really like about yourself.**

Of these two quotes about Trust, my favorite is by:

_____

My reason why is:

_____

_____

_____

My Big Answer - **The three things I really like about myself are:**

_____

_____

_____

My reason why:

_____

_____

_____

I will tell my friends, parents and other caring adults what I like about them!

Initial if yes: _____ Date: ____/____/_____ *If you selected yes, go to the pages starting on 110.*

When you complete it, come back and put the date you accomplished it here: ____/____/_____

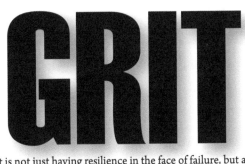

GRIT

"Grit is not just having resilience in the face of failure, but also having deep commitments that you remain loyal to over many years."

– *Deborah Perkins-Gough*
   Author, Senior Editor - Association for Supervision and Curriculum Development

Henry Ford once said, "If you do what you have always done, you'll get what you always got." I too, learned the hard way in life that, that's like sitting in a rocking chair; you're keeping busy, but getting nowhere. The key is to have grit and a growth mindset, like Henry Ford, and to keep trying new ways - that may take us out of our comfort zones - and adapating to grow."

– *Jim Cantoni - Realizing Dreams Founder and Author*

The BIG Question:
They say laughter is the best medicine, what makes you laugh?

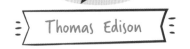

Thomas Edison

Of these two quotes about GRIT, my favorite is by:

_____

My reason why is:

_____

_____

_____

My Big Answer - **What makes me laugh is:**

_____

_____

_____

My reason why it makes me laugh is:

_____

_____

_____

I will use laughter as "medicine" to help myself and others in my own little way.

Initial if yes: _____ Date: ____/____/_____ *If you selected yes, go to the pages starting on 110.*

When you complete it, come back and put the date you accomplished it here: ____/____/_____

Character

"Character cannot be developed in ease and quiet. Only through experience of trial and suffering can the soul be strengthened, ambition inspired, and success achieved."

— *Helen Keller (1880 -1968)*

"Character may be manifested in the great moments, but it is made in the small ones."

— *Phillips Brooks (1835 - 1893)*
Author of O' Little Town of Bethlehem

The BIG Question:

If you were free to spend one year doing whatever you wanted to do, what would you do and why?

Of these two quotes about Character, my favorite is by:

_____

My reason why is:

_____

_____

_____

My Big Answer - **If I was free to spend one year doing what I wanted to do it would be:**

_____

_____

_____

My reason why:

_____

_____

_____

Here I set a goal to achieve this! I will create and implement my action plan.

Initial if yes: _____ Date: ____/____/_____ *If you selected yes, go to the pages starting on 110.*

When you complete it, come back and put the date you accomplished it here: ____/____/_____

Communication

Communication
Communication Communication

"True interactivity is not about clicking on icons or downloading files, it's about encouraging communication."

— *Edwin Schlossberg*
Internationally recognized Designer, Author and Artist

"Listen with the intent to understand, not reply."

— *Unknown*

The BIG Question:

What is one of your favorite family traditions or things to do as a family?

Of these two quotes about Communication, my favorite is by:

_____

My reason why:

_____

_____

_____

My Big Answer - **One of my favorite family traditions or things to do as a family is:** _____

_____

_____

My reason why:

_____

_____

_____

I would like to do this again.

Initial if yes: _____ Date: ____/____/_____ *If you selected yes, go to the pages starting on 110.*

When you complete it, come back and put the date you accomplished it here: ____/____/_____

Creativity

"An essential aspect of creativity is not being afraid to fail."

— *Edwin Land (1909 - 1991)*
Scientist and Inventor

"Creativity is a great motivator because it makes people interested in what they are doing. Creativity gives hope that there can be a worthwhile idea. Creativity gives the possibility of some sort of achievement to everyone. Creativity makes life more fun and interesting."

— *Edward de Bono*
British Physician, Inventor and Author

The BIG Question:

Are you afraid of anything? If so, what?

Of these two quotes about Creativity, my favorite is by:

_____

My reason why is:

_____

_____

_____

My Big Answer - I am afraid of:

_____

_____

_____

My reason why am afraid is:

_____

_____

_____

I think I can overcome this fear on my own, if not I will ask for help from people with experience that I trust.

Initial if yes: _____ Date: ____/____/_____ *If you selected yes, go to the pages starting on 110.*

When you complete it, come back and put the date you accomplished it here: ____/____/_____

Appreciating Diversity

"Diversity:
the art of thinking independently together."

— *Malcolm Forbes (1919 - 1940)*
Former Publisher of Forbes Magazine

"We need to give each other the space to
grow, to be ourselves, to exercise our diversity.
We need to give each other space so that we
may both give and receive such beautiful
things as ideas, openness, dignity, joy, healing,
and inclusion."

— *Max DePree, Author of Leadership is an Art*

The BIG Question:

**If you could choose any career and be
successful, (ie. a movie star, professional
athlete, medical doctor, school teacher)
what would it be and why?**

Of these two quotes about Diversity, my favorite is by: *De Pree*

My reason why is:

More comprehensive

My Big Answer - **I would choose to be one of these (or my dream is to be):**

Where I am right this minute

My reason why:

because on the best days, I am changing the lives of 24,000 children! I am changing the world!

Here I set a goal to become this! So that I accomplish it quicker and easier, I will use my energy by reading and learning from the experience of other successful people.

Initial if yes: *✓* Date: *3/27/19* *If you selected yes, go to the pages starting on 110.*

When you complete it, come back and put the date you accomplished it here: *3/27/19*

Helpfulness

"It is obvious that man is himself a traveler; that the purpose of this world is not 'to have and to hold' but 'to give and serve.' There can be no other meaning."

— Sir Wilfred T. Grenfell
Medical Missionary

"The service you do for others is the rent you pay for the time you spend on earth."

— Mohammed Ali

The BIG Question:

What movie have you seen more than once? Why?

Of these two quotes about Helpfulness, my favorite is by:

_____

My reason why is:

_____

_____

_____

My Big Answer - **The movie I have seen more than once is:**

_____

_____

_____

My reason why is:

_____

_____

_____

Some day, I will create a movie of something positive that has inspired me and share the inspiration with others.

Initial if yes: _____ Date: ____/____/_____ *If you selected yes, go to the pages starting on 110.*

When you complete it, come back and put the date you accomplished it here: ____/____/_____

HONESTY

"All profess honesty as long as they can. To believe all honest would be folly. To believe none so is something worse."

— *John Quincy Adams (1767 - 1848)*

"Honesty prospers in every condition of life."

— *Friedrich Schiller (1759 - 1805)*
Poet, Philosopher, and Historian

The BIG Question:

What are some qualities or characteristics you think are important in a friend?

Of these two quotes about Honesty, my favorite is by:

_____

My reason why is:

_____

_____

_____

My Big Answer - **The qualities or characteristics I think are important in a friend are:**

_____

_____

_____

My reason why:

_____

_____

_____

I personally will be a positive role model for these qualities and characteristics as well.

Initial if yes: _____ Date: ____/____/_____ _If you selected yes, go to the pages starting on 110._

When you complete it, come back and put the date you accomplished it here: ____/____/_____

Leadership

"The only real training for leadership is leadership."
— *Antony Jay, Author*

"Men make history, and not the other way around. In periods where there is no leadership, society stands still. Progress occurs when courageous, skillful leaders seize the opportunity to change things for the better."
— *Harry S. Truman (1884 - 1972)*

The BIG Question: **If you were asked to teach anything, what would you teach?**

Of these two quotes about Leadership, my favorite is by:

_____

My reason why is:

_____

_____

_____

My Big Answer - **If I was asked to teach something it would be:**

_____

_____

_____

My reason why:

_____

_____

_____

Someday, I will teach this and share this gift given to me with others in need.

Initial if yes: _____ Date: _____/_____/_____ *If you selected yes, go to the pages starting on 110.*

When you complete it, come back and put the date you accomplished it here: _____/_____/_____

Give a positive attitude ...
Get a
Positive
Attitude

— GivaGeta™

"Why are we the masters of our fate, the captains of our souls? Because we have the power to control our thoughts and our attitudes. That is why many people live in the withering negative world. That is why many people live in the positive attitude world. And you don't have to be a poet or a philosopher to know which is best."

— Alfred A. Montapert
Author

"Leadership is practiced not so much in words as in attitude and in actions."

— Harold Geneen (1910 - 1997)
Former President,
ITT Corporation

The BIG Question: **If you could only eat one food for an entire month, which food would you choose and why?**

Of these two quotes about a Positive Attitude, my favorite is by:

_____

My reason why is:

_____

_____

_____

My Big Answer - **The food I would eat for an entire month if I could only eat that is:**

_____

_____

_____

My reason why:

_____

_____

_____

I wouldn't really eat one food all month as it would not be healthy, but someday I will find a way to get food for others who are less fortunate than I.

Initial if yes: _____ Date: ____/____/_____ *If you selected yes, go to the pages starting on 110.*

When you complete it, come back and put the date you accomplished it here: ____/____/_____

Respect

"One of the most sincere forms of respect is actually listening to what another has to say."

— *Bryant H. McGill*
American Editor and Author

"When you are content to be simply yourself and don't compare or compete, everybody will respect you."

— *Lao Tzu, Ancient Chinese Philospher*

The BIG Question:

What is one of the funniest things that happened to you or someone you know?

Of these two quotes about Respect, my favorite is by:

_____

My reason why is:

_____

_____

_____

My Big Answer - **The funniest thing that happened to me or someone I know is:**

_____

_____

_____

My reason why I thought it was funny is:

_____

_____

_____

I will bring positive humor into other peoples' lives that I care about.

Initial if yes: _____ Date: ____/____/_____ *If you selected yes, go to the pages starting on 110.*

When you complete it, come back and put the date you accomplished it here: ____/____/_____

Responsibility

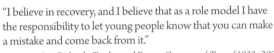

"I believe in recovery, and I believe that as a role model I have the responsibility to let young people know that you can make a mistake and come back from it."

– Ann Richards, Teacher and Former Governor of Texas (1933 - 2006)

"Whether a man is burdened by power or enjoys power; whether he is trapped by responsibility or made free by it; whether he is moved by other people and outer forces or moves them – this is of the essence of leadership."

– Theodore H. White (1915 - 1986)
Author of The Making of the President, 1960

The BIG Question:

What is (was) your favorite childhood toy?

Of these two quotes about Responsibility, my favorite is by:

_____

My reason why is:

_____

_____

_____

My Big Answer - **My favorite childhood toy is/was:**

_____

_____

_____

My reason why:

_____

_____

_____

Someday, I will help bring toys like the one I enjoyed to other children.

Initial if yes: _____ Date: ____/____/_____ *If you selected yes, go to the pages starting on 110.*

When you complete it, come back and put the date you accomplished it here: ____/____/_____

Teamwork

"The best teamwork comes from men who are working independently toward one goal in unison."

> — *James Cash Penney (1875 - 1971)*
> *Founder of J.C. Penney*

"Unity is strength ... when there is teamwork and collaboration, wonderful things can be achieved."

> — *Mattie Stepanek (1990 - 2004)*
> *American Poet and Advocate*

The BIG Question:

If you could visit any place in the world, where would you go and why?

Of these two quotes about Teamwork, my favorite is by:

_____

My reason why is:

_____

_____

_____

My Big Answer - **If I could visit any place in the world, it would be:**

_____

_____

_____

My reason why:

_____

_____

_____

Here I set a goal to go there! I will learn more by reading about it and sharing my goal with a caring adult.

Initial if yes: _____ Date: ____/____/_____ *If you selected yes, go to the pages starting on 110.*

When you complete it, come back and put the date you accomplished it here: ____/____/____

"Put more trust in nobility of character than in an oath."

— *Solon (638 BC - 559 BC)*
Athenian Statesman, Lawmaker, and Lyric Poet

"You may be deceived if you trust too much, but you will live in torment if you do not trust enough."

— *Frank Crane (1861 - 1928)*
Author of Everyday Wisdom

The BIG Question:

Who is one of your favorite TV or movie characters – real or cartoon - and why?

Of these two quotes about Trust, my favorite is by:

_____

My reason why is:

_____

_____

_____

My Big Answer - **One of my favorite TV character (real or cartoon) is:**

_____

_____

_____

My reason why:

_____

_____

_____

I will give the same joy from this character I get from this to another child!

Initial if yes: _____ Date: _____/_____/_____ *If you selected yes, go to the pages starting on 110.*

When you complete it, come back and put the date you accomplished it here: _____/_____/_____

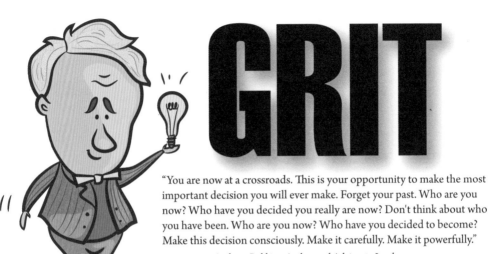

GRIT

Thomas Edison

"You are now at a crossroads. This is your opportunity to make the most important decision you will ever make. Forget your past. Who are you now? Who have you decided you really are now? Don't think about who you have been. Who are you now? Who have you decided to become? Make this decision consciously. Make it carefully. Make it powerfully."

– Anthony Robbins, Author and Advisor to Leaders

The Little Engine That Could has GRIT ... "I think I can, I think I can."

– Jim Cantoni
Realizing Dreams Founder and Author

The BIG Question:
What are one or two things you are most excited about?

Of these two quotes about GRIT, my favorite is by:

_____

My reason why is:

_____

_____

_____

My Big Answer - I am most excited about:

_____

_____

_____

My reason why:

_____

_____

_____

I will use this excitement to empower myself and others in my own special way.

Initial if yes: _____ Date: ____/____/_____ *If you selected yes, go to the pages starting on 110.*

When you complete it, come back and put the date you accomplished it here: ____/____/_____

"Intelligence plus character
- that is the goal of true education."

- Dr. Martin Luther King, Jr.

21st Century Life Skill Assets™
For High School, College, and Career Success

Self-Assessment: On the next page you will see a self-reflection activity that was created to help you discover yourself in greater ways.

For this activity, take a few moments to reflect on your strengths and think of your Top 5 greatest character traits. Next, put #1 above what you feel is your greatest character trait. Then in order, number the next with #2, #3, #4 and #5.

As another activity for real self-discovery, select your "RFI's", which are the "Room For Improvements". These are the character traits you know you can get better at. As a suggestion, you could read the quotes again for inspiration and challenge yourself with one character trait of the day, week or month to focus on. This would not only make you, but Benjamin Franklin proud. As the story goes, good old Ben had a list of 12 virtues he worked on too. I often say we all have the same room - room for improvement, that is!

Feedback: Ask a caring and trusted adult what they think your greatest strengths are on the following page and, most importantly, why they think so. This would be great practice for a job interview when the prospective employer asks your greatest strengths. As an E²™ power life tip, make sure that a Positive Attitude is in your Top 5, if not your #1.

Self-Assessment and Feedback

(see prior page for instructions) Of these 13 positive character traits, my **Top 5** and **greatest strengths** are:

GRIT

"Your dreams are on the other side of your grit."
- *Reprinted in Pinterest by Abbie Lincoln Guidance Counselor, Spencer County Middle School*

"People who can set long-term goals and stick to them have a leg up on success in school and life. The most successful people in life are both talented and gritty in whatever they've chosen to do."
- *Deborah Perkins-Gough, Senior Editor Association for Supervision and Curriculum Development*

Thomas Edison

The BIG Question:
What is one thing that you are most worried about and why?

Character

"People grow through experience if they meet life honestly and courageously. This is how character is built."
- *Eleanor Roosevelt (1884–1962)*

"Character is forged in the smallest of struggles. Then, when the big challenges come, we're ready."
- *Walter Rand, Water Rand weblog, 12.30.05*

The BIG Question:
You have learned many things in life. What is one of the most useful?

Communication

"True interactivity is not about clicking on icons or downloading files, it's about encouraging communication."
- *Edwin Schlossberg Internationally recognized Designer, Author and Artist*

"Listen with the intent to understand, not reply."
- *Unknown*

The BIG Question:
What is one of your favorite family traditions or things to do as a family?

Creativity

"Creativity is the power to connect the seemingly unconnected."
- *William Plomer (1903–1973) South African Author, Novelist, Poet and Literary Editor*

"The problem is never how to get new, innovative thoughts into your mind, but how to get old ones out. Every mind is a building filled with archaic furniture. Clean out a corner of your mind and creativity will instantly fill it."
- *Dee Hock, Founder and Former CEO of VISA*

The BIG Question:
If you could be an eyewitness to any big event in history, what would it be and why?

Appreciating Diversity

"Diversity is the one true thing we all have in common. Celebrate it every day."
- *Anonymous*

"If we cannot end now our differences, at least we can help make the world safe for diversity."
- *John F. Kennedy (1917–1963)*

The BIG Question:
What is one thing you are learning to do well?

Helpfulness

"One day a small boy tried to lift a heavy stone, but couldn't budge it. His father, watching, finally said, 'Are you sure you're using all your strength?' 'Yes, I am!' the boy cried. 'No, you're not,' said the father. 'You haven't asked me to help you.'"
- *Unknown*

"All for one, one for all!"
- *The Three Musketeers*

The BIG Question:
If you could speak another language, which would you choose and what would you use it for?

HONESTY

"Where is there dignity unless there is honesty?"
- *Cicero, Philosopher*

"My motto –
first honesty, then industry, then concentration."
- *Andrew Carnegie (1835–1919) Founder of Carnegie Corporation*

The BIG Question:
If you could travel back in time or into the future, where would you go and why?

Thirteen 21st Century Life Skill Assets™
For Success in High School, College and Career

Leadership

"Leadership is communicating to people their worth and potential so clearly that they come to see it in themselves."
– Stephen Covey
Author of 7 Habits of Highly Effective People

"Give leadership ... Get dedication."
– GiveGetin™

The BIG Question: Who is one person you admire or look up to as a role model? What influence have they had in your life?

Give a positive attitude
Get a Positive Attitude

"The greatest discovery of my generation is that a human being can alter their life by altering their attitude."
– William James (1842-1910)
American Psychologist

"I am determined to be cheerful and happy in whatever situation I may be; for I have learned from experience that our happiness or misery depends upon our dispositions and not upon our circumstances."
– Martha Washington (1732-1802)
The first First Lady of the United States

The BIG Question: What would you do if you knew you could not fail?

Respect

"If you want to be respected by others, the great thing is to respect yourself. Only by that, only by self-respect will you compel others to respect you."
– Fyodor Dostoevsky (1821-1881)
Author

"Give respect ... Get respect."
– GiveGetin™

The BIG Question:
What is something you have always dreamed about doing?

Responsibility

"I believe that every right implies a responsibility; every opportunity, an obligation; every possession, a duty."
– J.D. Rockefeller (1839-1937)
American Industrialist and Philanthropist

"The more freedom we enjoy, the greater the responsibility we bear toward others as well as ourselves."
– Oscar Arias Sanchez
President of Costa Rica (2006-1987 Nobel Peace Prize)

The BIG Question:
Who is (or was) one of your friends in elementary school and what do you like about him or her?

Teamwork

"To succeed as a team is to hold all of the members accountable for their expertise."
– Mitchell Caplan, Former CEO of E*Trade Group Inc.

"Give teamwork ... Get results."
– GiveGetin™

The BIG Question:
If you could excel at any sport or activity, what would it be and why?

Trust yourself.
Create the kind of self that you will be happy to live with all your life.
Make the most of yourself by fanning the tiny, inner sparks of possibility into flames of achievement.
– Golda Meir (1898-1978)
Former Prime Minister of Israel

"I know God will not give me anything I can't handle. I just wish that He didn't trust me so much."
– Mother Teresa (1910 - 1997)

The BIG Question:
What is one of the funniest outfits or costumes you or someone you know ever wore?

My Declaration to Realize My Dreams in Life:

Date (enter today's date) initials (put your initials here). Write down the details:

My Goal is from page (enter page #) **or** (check if from) **my Dream Tag™.**

EXAMPLE ONLY
GO to page 112 to complete your first one

Specific _____ What do you want to accomplish? _____

Measurable How will you know that you did it? _____

Attainable Do you think you can? Remember what Henry Ford said, "Whether you think you can, or think you can't you are right." Which way do you want to think, you can or you can't? What can you research or read to equip and empower yourself to accomplish this? _____

Relevant _____ Why is this something you really want in life? _____

Time Bound By what date will you accomplish this? _____

Remember: Visualize. **I**nternalize. **A**ctualize.

See it, feel it, believe it and you will achieve it!

Here is a picture of what my dream and GETTING SMARTR™ goal looks like:

My Next steps are: ***EXAMPLE ONLY*** GO to page 112 to complete your first one

	By When	Date Accomplished	Check When Completed
1.	___/___/___	___/___/___	✓
2.	___/___/___	___/___/___	☐
3.	___/___/___	___/___/___	☐
4.	___/___/___	___/___/___	☐
5.	___/___/___	___/___/___	☐
6.	___/___/___	___/___/___	☐
7.	___/___/___	___/___/___	☐
8.	___/___/___	___/___/___	☐
9.	___/___/___	___/___/___	☐
10.	___/___/___	___/___/___	☐

My Declaration to Realize My Dreams in Life:

Date _3/27/19_ Initials _RB_ Write down the details:

My Goal is from page _87_ or _____ from my Dream Tag™. It is:

Specific _In there now_

Measurable _I am Progress_

Attainable _Yes_

Relevant _Absolutely for the path_

Time Bound _By 1 year._

Remember: **V**isualize. **I**nternalize. **A**ctualize.

See it, feel it, believe it and you will achieve it!

Here is a picture of what my dream and GETTING SMARTR™ goal looks like:

Sig for all

REALIZING
★ Dreams ★
Engage. Equip. Empower.™

My Next steps are:

1. Principal Acceptance
2. Regionals
3. Presentation
4. Overcoming Objection
5. GCC Hurdles
6. Faculty adaptation
7. Inf of ECE
8. College P'ways
9.
10.

By When	Date Accomplished	Check When Completed
/ /	/ /	☐
/ /	/ /	☐
/ /	/ /	☐
/ /	/ /	☐
/ /	/ /	☐
/ /	/ /	☐
/ /	/ /	☐
/ /	/ /	☐

My Declaration to Realize My Dreams in Life:

Date _____ Initials _____ Write down the details:

My Goal is from page _____ or _____ from my Dream Tag™. It is:

Specific _____

Measurable _____

Attainable _____

Relevant _____

Time Bound _____

Remember: Visualize. **I**nternalize. **A**ctualize.

See it, feel it, believe it and you will achieve it!

Here is a picture of what my dream and GETTING SMARTR™ goal looks like:

My Next steps are:

	By When	Date Accomplished	Check When Completed
1.	___/___/_____	___/___/_____	☐
2.	___/___/_____	___/___/_____	☐
3.	___/___/_____	___/___/_____	☐
4.	___/___/_____	___/___/_____	☐
5.	___/___/_____	___/___/_____	☐
6.	___/___/_____	___/___/_____	☐
7.	___/___/_____	___/___/_____	☐
8.	___/___/_____	___/___/_____	☐
9.	___/___/_____	___/___/_____	☐
10.	___/___/_____	___/___/_____	☐

My Declaration to Realize My Dreams in Life:

Date _____ Initials _____ Write down the details:

My Goal is from page _____ or _____ from my Dream Tag™. It is:

Specific _____

Measurable _____

Attainable _____

Relevant _____

Time Bound _____

Remember: Visualize. **I**nternalize. **A**ctualize.

See it, feel it, believe it and you will achieve it!

Here is a picture of what my dream and GETTING SMARTR™ goal looks like:

My Next steps are:

	By When	Date Accomplished	Check When Completed
1.	___/___/_____	___/___/_____	☐
2.	___/___/_____	___/___/_____	☐
3.	___/___/_____	___/___/_____	☐
4.	___/___/_____	___/___/_____	☐
5.	___/___/_____	___/___/_____	☐
6.	___/___/_____	___/___/_____	☐
7.	___/___/_____	___/___/_____	☐
8.	___/___/_____	___/___/_____	☐
9.	___/___/_____	___/___/_____	☐
10.	___/___/_____	___/___/_____	☐

My Declaration to Realize My Dreams in Life:

Date _____ Initials _____ Write down the details:

My Goal is from page _____ or _____ from my Dream Tag™. It is:

Specific _____

Measurable _____

Attainable _____

Relevant _____

Time Bound _____

Remember: Visualize. **I**nternalize. **A**ctualize.

See it, feel it, believe it and you will achieve it!

Here is a picture of what my dream and GETTING SMARTR™ goal looks like:

My Next steps are:

	By When	Date Accomplished	Check When Completed
1.	___/___/_____	___/___/_____	☐
2.	___/___/_____	___/___/_____	☐
3.	___/___/_____	___/___/_____	☐
4.	___/___/_____	___/___/_____	☐
5.	___/___/_____	___/___/_____	☐
6.	___/___/_____	___/___/_____	☐
7.	___/___/_____	___/___/_____	☐
8.	___/___/_____	___/___/_____	☐
9.	___/___/_____	___/___/_____	☐
10.	___/___/_____	___/___/_____	☐

My Declaration to Realize My Dreams in Life:

Date _____ Initials _____ Write down the details:

My Goal is from page _____ or _____ from my Dream Tag™. It is:

Specific _____

Measurable _____

Attainable _____

Relevant _____

Time Bound _____

Remember: Visualize. **I**nternalize. **A**ctualize.

See it, feel it, believe it and you will achieve it!

Here is a picture of what my dream and GETTING SMARTR™ goal looks like:

My Next steps are:

	By When	Date Accomplished	Check When Completed
1.	___/___/_____	___/___/_____	☐
2.	___/___/_____	___/___/_____	☐
3.	___/___/_____	___/___/_____	☐
4.	___/___/_____	___/___/_____	☐
5.	___/___/_____	___/___/_____	☐
6.	___/___/_____	___/___/_____	☐
7.	___/___/_____	___/___/_____	☐
8.	___/___/_____	___/___/_____	☐
9.	___/___/_____	___/___/_____	☐
10.	___/___/_____	___/___/_____	☐

My Declaration to Realize My Dreams in Life:

Date _____ Initials _____ Write down the details:

My Goal is from page _____ or _____ from my Dream Tag™. It is:

Specific _____

Measurable _____

Attainable _____

Relevant _____

Time Bound _____

Remember: Visualize. **I**nternalize. **A**ctualize.

See it, feel it, believe it and you will achieve it!

Here is a picture of what my dream and GETTING SMARTR™ goal looks like:

My Next steps are:

	By When	Date Accomplished	Check When Completed
1.	___/___/_____	___/___/_____	☐
2.	___/___/_____	___/___/_____	☐
3.	___/___/_____	___/___/_____	☐
4.	___/___/_____	___/___/_____	☐
5.	___/___/_____	___/___/_____	☐
6.	___/___/_____	___/___/_____	☐
7.	___/___/_____	___/___/_____	☐
8.	___/___/_____	___/___/_____	☐
9.	___/___/_____	___/___/_____	☐
10.	___/___/_____	___/___/_____	☐

My Declaration to Realize My Dreams in Life:

Date _____ Initials _____ Write down the details:

My Goal is from page _____ or _____ from my Dream Tag™. It is:

Specific _____

Measurable _____

Attainable _____

Relevant _____

Time Bound _____

Remember: Visualize. **I**nternalize. **A**ctualize.

See it, feel it, believe it and you will achieve it!

Here is a picture of what my dream and GETTING SMARTR™ goal looks like:

My Next steps are:

	By When	Date Accomplished	Check When Completed
1.	___/___/_____	___/___/_____	☐
2.	___/___/_____	___/___/_____	☐
3.	___/___/_____	___/___/_____	☐
4.	___/___/_____	___/___/_____	☐
5.	___/___/_____	___/___/_____	☐
6.	___/___/_____	___/___/_____	☐
7.	___/___/_____	___/___/_____	☐
8.	___/___/_____	___/___/_____	☐
9.	___/___/_____	___/___/_____	☐
10.	___/___/_____	___/___/_____	☐

My Declaration to Realize My Dreams in Life:

Date _____ Initials _____ Write down the details:

My Goal is from page _____ or _____ from my Dream Tag™. It is:

Specific _____

Measurable _____

Attainable _____

Relevant _____

Time Bound _____

Remember: Visualize. **I**nternalize. **A**ctualize.

See it, feel it, believe it and you will achieve it!

Here is a picture of what my dream and GETTING SMARTR™ goal looks like:

My Next steps are:

	By When	Date Accomplished	Check When Completed
1.	___/___/_____	___/___/_____	☐
2.	___/___/_____	___/___/_____	☐
3.	___/___/_____	___/___/_____	☐
4.	___/___/_____	___/___/_____	☐
5.	___/___/_____	___/___/_____	☐
6.	___/___/_____	___/___/_____	☐
7.	___/___/_____	___/___/_____	☐
8.	___/___/_____	___/___/_____	☐
9.	___/___/_____	___/___/_____	☐
10.	___/___/_____	___/___/_____	☐

My Declaration to Realize My Dreams in Life:

Date _____ Initials _____ Write down the details:

My Goal is from page _____ or _____ from my Dream Tag™. It is:

Specific _____

Measurable _____

Attainable _____

Relevant _____

Time Bound _____

Remember: Visualize. **I**nternalize. **A**ctualize.

See it, feel it, believe it and you will achieve it!

Here is a picture of what my dream and GETTING SMARTR™ goal looks like:

My Next steps are:

	By When	Date Accomplished	Check When Completed
1.	____/____/_____	____/____/_____	☐
2.	____/____/_____	____/____/_____	☐
3.	____/____/_____	____/____/_____	☐
4.	____/____/_____	____/____/_____	☐
5.	____/____/_____	____/____/_____	☐
6.	____/____/_____	____/____/_____	☐
7.	____/____/_____	____/____/_____	☐
8.	____/____/_____	____/____/_____	☐
9.	____/____/_____	____/____/_____	☐
10.	____/____/_____	____/____/_____	☐

My Declaration to Realize My Dreams in Life:

Date _____ Initials _____ Write down the details:

My Goal is from page _____ or _____ from my Dream Tag™. It is:

Specific _____

Measurable _____

Attainable _____

Relevant _____

Time Bound _____

Remember: Visualize. **I**nternalize. **A**ctualize.

See it, feel it, believe it and you will achieve it!

Here is a picture of what my dream and GETTING SMARTR™ goal looks like:

My Next steps are:

	By When	Date Accomplished	Check When Completed
1.	___/___/_____	___/___/_____	☐
2.	___/___/_____	___/___/_____	☐
3.	___/___/_____	___/___/_____	☐
4.	___/___/_____	___/___/_____	☐
5.	___/___/_____	___/___/_____	☐
6.	___/___/_____	___/___/_____	☐
7.	___/___/_____	___/___/_____	☐
8.	___/___/_____	___/___/_____	☐
9.	___/___/_____	___/___/_____	☐
10.	___/___/_____	___/___/_____	☐

My Declaration to Realize My Dreams in Life:

Date _____ Initials _____ Write down the details:

My Goal is from page _____ or _____ from my Dream Tag™. It is:

Specific _____

Measurable _____

Attainable _____

Relevant _____

Time Bound _____

Remember: Visualize. **I**nternalize. **A**ctualize.

See it, feel it, believe it and you will achieve it!

Here is a picture of what my dream and GETTING SMARTR™ goal looks like:

My Next steps are:

	By When	Date Accomplished	Check When Completed
1.	___/___/_____	___/___/_____	☐
2.	___/___/_____	___/___/_____	☐
3.	___/___/_____	___/___/_____	☐
4.	___/___/_____	___/___/_____	☐
5.	___/___/_____	___/___/_____	☐
6.	___/___/_____	___/___/_____	☐
7.	___/___/_____	___/___/_____	☐
8.	___/___/_____	___/___/_____	☐
9.	___/___/_____	___/___/_____	☐
10.	___/___/_____	___/___/_____	☐

My Declaration to Realize My Dreams in Life:

Date _____ Initials _____ Write down the details:

My Goal is from page _____ or _____ from my Dream Tag™. It is:

Specific _____

Measurable _____

Attainable _____

Relevant _____

Time Bound _____

Remember: Visualize. **I**nternalize. **A**ctualize.

See it, feel it, believe it and you will achieve it!

Here is a picture of what my dream and GETTING SMARTR™ goal looks like:

My Next steps are:

	By When	Date Accomplished	Check When Completed
1.	___/___/_____	___/___/_____	☐
2.	___/___/_____	___/___/_____	☐
3.	___/___/_____	___/___/_____	☐
4.	___/___/_____	___/___/_____	☐
5.	___/___/_____	___/___/_____	☐
6.	___/___/_____	___/___/_____	☐
7.	___/___/_____	___/___/_____	☐
8.	___/___/_____	___/___/_____	☐
9.	___/___/_____	___/___/_____	☐
10.	___/___/_____	___/___/_____	☐

My Declaration to Realize My Dreams in Life:

Date _____ Initials _____ Write down the details:

My Goal is from page _____ or _____ from my Dream Tag™. It is:

Specific _____

Measurable _____

Attainable _____

Relevant _____

Time Bound _____

Remember: Visualize. **I**nternalize. **A**ctualize.

See it, feel it, believe it and you will achieve it!

Here is a picture of what my dream and GETTING SMARTR™ goal looks like:

My Next steps are:

	By When	Date Accomplished	Check When Completed
1.	___/___/_____	___/___/_____	☐
2.	___/___/_____	___/___/_____	☐
3.	___/___/_____	___/___/_____	☐
4.	___/___/_____	___/___/_____	☐
5.	___/___/_____	___/___/_____	☐
6.	___/___/_____	___/___/_____	☐
7.	___/___/_____	___/___/_____	☐
8.	___/___/_____	___/___/_____	☐
9.	___/___/_____	___/___/_____	☐
10.	___/___/_____	___/___/_____	☐

My Declaration to Realize My Dreams in Life:

Date _____ Initials _____ Write down the details:

My Goal is from page _____ or _____ from my Dream Tag™. It is:

Specific _____

Measurable _____

Attainable _____

Relevant _____

Time Bound _____

Remember: Visualize. **I**nternalize. **A**ctualize.

See it, feel it, believe it and you will achieve it!

Here is a picture of what my dream and GETTING SMARTR™ goal looks like:

My Next steps are:

	By When	Date Accomplished	Check When Completed
1.	___/___/_____	___/___/_____	☐
2.	___/___/_____	___/___/_____	☐
3.	___/___/_____	___/___/_____	☐
4.	___/___/_____	___/___/_____	☐
5.	___/___/_____	___/___/_____	☐
6.	___/___/_____	___/___/_____	☐
7.	___/___/_____	___/___/_____	☐
8.	___/___/_____	___/___/_____	☐
9.	___/___/_____	___/___/_____	☐
10.	___/___/_____	___/___/_____	☐

My Declaration to Realize My Dreams in Life:

Date _____ Initials _____ Write down the details:

My Goal is from page _____ or _____ from my Dream Tag™. It is:

Specific _____

Measurable _____

Attainable _____

Relevant _____

Time Bound _____

Remember: Visualize. **I**nternalize. **A**ctualize.

See it, feel it, believe it and you will achieve it!

Here is a picture of what my dream and GETTING SMARTR™ goal looks like:

My Next steps are:

	By When	Date Accomplished	Check When Completed
1.	___/___/_____	___/___/_____	☐
2.	___/___/_____	___/___/_____	☐
3.	___/___/_____	___/___/_____	☐
4.	___/___/_____	___/___/_____	☐
5.	___/___/_____	___/___/_____	☐
6.	___/___/_____	___/___/_____	☐
7.	___/___/_____	___/___/_____	☐
8.	___/___/_____	___/___/_____	☐
9.	___/___/_____	___/___/_____	☐
10.	___/___/_____	___/___/_____	☐

"I want to recruit character-large people."

– Coach Assaiante
  Winningest Coach in College Sports
  Trinity College Mens' Squash Coach
  13 straight National Championships
  252 straight wins
  Author, Run to the Roar

My Faves:

My Favorite Inspirational quote is on page _____

My Favorite of The BIG Questions is on page _____

My Greatest Character Strengths are on pages _____

My #1 Character Strength is _____

My Favorite Self-Efficacy Formula is _____

My #1 Dream in life is on page _____

My #2 Dream in life is on page _____

My #3 Dream in life is on page _____

My #4 Dream in life is on page _____

My #5 Dream in life is on page _____

Post your "My Faves" on our:

 Facebook/RealizingDreams.us   Twitter @MissionUSA2020

For More Self-Discovery Fun...

1. For thought-provoking, intergenerational fun, ask your family, friends or relatives to take turns reading and answering The BIG Questions and quotes together.

2. Re-read the inspirational quotes and reflect on how you can apply them in your daily life at home, in school, with friends and in your community.

3. If *7 Steps for EMPOWERING YOUTH* has inspired you and you want to help get the word out, here are four thought starters: 1) Tell your friends 2) Share with your teachers or other positive youth development organizations and use it for a very meaningful and powerful School-Family Reading night. 3) Submit your success stories to a local or national news organization like USA Today 4) Share your story with your friends and us on social media! We are on Twitter at @MissionUSA2020 and www.Facebook.com/RealizingDreams.us.

4. If you didn't purchase *7 Steps for EMPOWERING YOUTH* in The Student Dream Kit™ edition, visit www.RealizingDreams.us to pick up the game edition. This fun-filled game version contains 12 activities for family and community building. The small to large group hands-on team activities include meaningful discussion starters with The BIG Questions like in this book, as well as building card towers like in the photo at left. You'll develop your GRIT, learn to solve problems and overcome challenges for a growth mindset in a way that connects 21st century learning to the real world. *And oh yeah, to make it even more FUN, throw down some team challenges!*

5. To see your progress review your goals you've set and accomplished! Revisit your Self-Assessment and Feedback page. Reflect on "My Top 5 Character Strengths" after you complete *7 Steps for EMPOWERING YOUTH,* your self-discovery LifeBook.

Why the Book's Name Change?

A note from the author, Jim Cantoni and Founder of Realizing Dreams

To better reflect the outcomes after two+ years of piloting the book *Teamwork and FamilyPlay - Empowering youth through self-discovery,* and only two months before printing 11,000 copies, it was two children, 6 and 8 years old and four youth development experts who gratefully inspired me to change the name of this "self-discovery Lifebook" to *7 Steps for EMPOWERING YOUTH - Self-awareness developing Grit and a Growth Mindset.*

"This will never make me give up"

Based on research, understanding, years of testing and personally facilitating over 200 positive youth development workshops, the renaming of the book became clear after one very powerful seed was planted while I was facilitating a youth empowerment workshop on Friday, April 17, 2015. Just like a lot of things in life, at times, we do not connect the dots initially unless we trust our gut instincts and let them grow. That is what happened after seeing what eight year old Andrew wrote in his lifebook about his favorite trait, CREATIVITY. He also selected and reflected on his favorite quote, by William Plomer, that *"Creativity is the power to connect the seemingly unconnected."* In writing, *"This will never make me give up,"* Andrew defined "GRIT" in a simple and very powerful way. South African author and poet, William Plomer, is surely smiling knowing that he inspired creativity, perseverance and grit in our youth. As shown on my Facebook page for the last few years, William Plomer's creativity quote is one of my favorites too. Many people who know me, also know that I don't give up too easily.

"Are we raising kids who don't know how to dream big dreams?" This is what I call one of "The BIG Questions" in life. It was posed by Dr. Carol Dweck in her remarkable Ted Talks, *The Power of Believing That You Can Improve.* Dr. Dweck is a renowned Stanford University psychologist and the author of *Mindset: The New Psychology of Success.*

Dreaming big dreams and clearly seeing your path to a successful future.
On that same Friday, more seeds to rename the book grew from Andrew's six year old sister Kathryn. In her copy of the earlier edition of this book, Kathryn was inspired to set three short term goals: sing, practice, and sing to her parents on Mother's Day - which was just 3 weeks away.

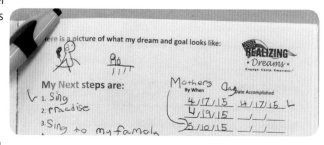

However, it was what I saw next that blew me away! At only six years old, Kathryn was dreaming big dreams! She drew a picture and wrote her long term goal to be a judge on American idol by the time she is 30 years old. Kathryn clearly sees her path to a successful future as the picture she drew illustrates her long-term goal that is 24 years away!

"Know thyself." – **Socrates.** More inspiration arrived that Tuesday, only four days, later after my newfound understanding about "Grit and a Growth Mindset". The seed of William Plomer's wisdom of creativity, being the power to connect the seemingly unconnected, continued to grow from a connection a month earlier. This connection came from an introduction by Noel Pardo, Operations Director at Tabor Academy Summer Program. Noel gratefully believed in me and in the summer of 2014, took a leadership role as his camp was one of the first to pilot Realizing Dreams. After the successful outcomes, Noel introduced me to Troy Bennett, University of Utah College of Health - Parks, Recreation, and Tourism Department and Research Assistant at the American Camp Association.

"As we look ahead into the next century, leaders will be those who empower others."

– Bill Gates, Founder of Microsoft

With Troy, I shared the steps I use to empower youth and the stories of Andrew and Kathryn, where they voiced their passions and learned how to set and achieve goals to realize their dreams in life. Troy helped me more clearly understand the research. I now know why my book and business, called Realizing Dreams, successfully empowers youth and develops grit and a growth mindset. Troy shared that, according to the review [The impact of non-cognitive skills on outcomes for young people, Literature review, 21 November 2013, Institute of Education, Leslie Morrison Gutman, Ingrid], perseverance is related to one's ability to achieve long-term goals. Perseverance consists of two parts - grit and engagement. Realizing Dreams is successful because it engages kids and helps them develop the ability to achieve their goals. By engaging kids in goal achievement, Realizing Dreams contributes to the development of Grit and a Growth Mindset where youth believe that they can improve and get better. I think Duckworth et al. refer to it mostly in education

- one's belief that they can get smarter - that your intelligence can grow - as opposed to kids, that may be economically disadvantaged, who at times, may think they are not as smart as others and that is just the way it is."

Don't give up, "Not Yet". The research on self-control and GRIT by Dr. Angela Duckworth and the research on growth mindset and "Not Yet" by Dr. Carol Dweck shows that we all have the power to improve if we believe that we can. It also shows that if we ever feel, "not as smart", believe, "not yet, anyway". I truly believe that any of us can change if we are equipped with these and the self-efficacy Life Skills Assets™ to never give up, to "Be in the 3%", set GETTING SMARTR™ goals as this lifebook shows, but most of all, believe we can like *The Little Engine That Could - "I think I can, I think I can"*.

"It's not that I'm so smart; it's just that I stay with problems longer." – Einstein
So whether it is a judge on a talent show or whatever your big dream is, the essence of setting long term goals even as early as age six like Kathryn, and learning to never give up like her brother Andrew both teach us are secrets to life. We all have the creativity to connect the seemingly unconnected. When we adapt, we will get better and then realize our dreams when we stay with our problems long enough - *just like Einstein.*

Needless to say, I am totally grateful for the life experiences from youth like you, Kathryn and Andrew whose stories further inspire and empower me. As well as the youth development experts like you, Noel and Troy, and the researchers like Dr. Duckworth and Dr. Dweck who helped me realize that a better name for this book is the *7 Steps for EMPOWERING YOUTH*: **Self-Awareness Developing GRIT and a Growth Mindset.** My 12+ years of experience combined with several years of testing and piloting has found that this self-discovery "LifeBook" synchronizes generations and engages, equips and empowers youth with predictors of success.

Afterword:
More about you, this "LifeBook", and Me

Give inspiration ... Get inspired™ is one of my favorite "GivaGeta" messages. So, for those interested in inspiring others, here is a little more about you, this LifeBook and me.

Picture yourself 5, 10 or 25 years ahead in the future. What do you see? Success, joy, happiness and fulfillment? Do you see yourself as a software engineer, a doctor, a writer, a professional athlete or as a life coach who inspires potential in others?

Whatever your dreams are, I hope *7 Steps for EMPOWERING YOUTH* engaged, equipped and empowered you to find and see your pathway to reach your full potential, realize your dreams and achieve greater life outcomes.

By completing your LifeBook, you should have become more self-aware and seen your new strengths and self-efficacy Life Skill Assets™ materialize in front of your eyes. Always reflect on your positive qualities so that you can continue to develop them and make them really come alive. We all have the same room– that is room for improvement. The most important thing is to be open minded, have a positive attitude and be receptive to making changes to better your life.

My hope is that you consider this book your life's playbook. I hope it becomes one of your best friends, a keepsake, and memory time capsule of your life at this point in time. Re-read it. Reflect on your accomplishments and when you wrote them. Revisit it every time you start to question who you are and what you want to be. When you need a little pick me up, another hope is that it will renew your energy and re-inspire you to carry on even during life's challenging twists and turns. I hope you enjoyed the engaging activities devoted to the person you are and the person you can be.

Realize Dreams In Teams™ Share *7 Steps for EMPOWERING YOUTH* with those adults– parents, foster parents, grandparents, aunts, uncles, teachers, counselors, mentors, guardians and other caring adults– who mean a lot to you. They will learn about your hopes, interests, dreams, goals, fears, worries and aspirations. Synchronize your energy and their experience so you learn the easier way in school, work, life, health and play. Ask them to help you realize your dreams. Then, if you ever have children, share it with them and inspire your children to share it with their children so everyone is on a path to successful futures.

Who and what was the inspiration for 7 Steps for EMPOWERING YOUTH?
While I was facilitating a leadership workshop in New Jersey in 2009 with this book's cousin, the Teamwork and TeamPlay the active learning game edition (created in 2008 in collaboration with the great Dr. Jim Cain), a Girl Scout leader and grandmother of 16 grandchildren purchased a set. She wanted her family to get off their phones and computers so that they could play, talk, interact and have fun the way she remembered. She inspired me to create a game to do just that. Teamwork and FamilyPlay was designed to be a fun family and community building game with problem solving and educational leadership activities for students, parents, teachers, mentors, and everyone in between.

A Seal of Approval - In August 2011, The National Parenting Center awarded the game edition of Teamwork and FamilyPlay (on which this *7 Steps for EMPOWERING YOUTH* is based) their Seal of Approval. Their appraisal of the game speaks volumes: *"Geared for families with children of all ages, our testers gave great reviews to this very unique and ambitious game. Game may not be the*

best term for Teamwork and FamilyPlay as what it really did was get families talking and sharing like never before. Families reported learning interesting things about one another that they never knew before. Let's face it teens and pre-teens aren't always the most open when it comes to conversations with their parents. These cards found a way to bridge the divide and get real conversations started. Each card is loaded with fun activities, many of them based on the pillars of Character Counts. Parents like that there were often brain teasers that required some serious thought about completing each activity. This would also be wonderful for leaders of Scouts, church groups and the like."

Then, about a year and a half later in February 2013, while organizing my bookcase, I saw one of my favorite little books called <u>Life's Little Instruction Book - Volume II</u> by H. Jackson Brown, Jr. Suddenly, an inspiring thought popped into my head: *What if I transformed the game edition into a self-discovery and personal "little workbook" to synchronize generations and transform lives like I do in my workshops?* Since this book is all about self-discovery and mindful self-awareness of our hopes, dreams, and goals in life, I decided to call this a "LifeBook" as it is part book and part workbook all about your life.

7 Steps for EMPOWERING YOUTH also uses several "self-efficacy" formulas, including ME^2™, which is "Meaningful Enrichment all about ME" and learning the easy way to increase your success in life. I surely learned some of life's lessons the hard way a few years ago. From the time I was 48 until I reached 53, life sent me through some pretty tough twists and turns with serious health challenges and more. Undoubtedly, those were some of the most challenging years of my life. Although they were difficult, they were learning years. I re-discovered myself and learned how to focus and engage on what is important.

Through learning and refocusing on what was truly important for my family and me, I discovered that I could help others. **My hope was to teach others how to engage, equip, and empower themselves with the social and emotional intelligence "Life Skill Assets" to overcome obstacles in life.** The Life Skill Assets™ include: keeping a positive attitude, having the ability to listen with the intent to understand, setting GETTING SMARTR™ goals early in life, being self-aware, having GRIT, and believing you can improve with a growth mindset to help you overcome future obstacles.

I had to put this to work in my own life when, after a serious accident at age 24, I was left blind in one eye. Another serious injury at 32 left me disabled and out of work, which was a very humbling experience. Needless to say, I didn't always have such a positive outlook during those trying times. At age 40, I was inspired by another book and I found my way back to looking ahead to the future with focus and self-empowerment. I could do anything once again. I want my story and my experience of learning the hard way to help you to learn the easy way. I want you to save time and not waste your precious years. I believe that you can realize your dreams early in life—*starting now.*

Collective Impact: An Einstein Inspired Invitation

This is the 4th edition, however as I made the final edits to the 3rd edition in April 2014 and I reflected on the news headlines over the last several years showing the United States of America's education, income and health challenges. I now even more believe that we need to follow what Mr. Brian Gallagher, CEO of United Way Worldwide inspires us to do with his 2012 *Charting A Course For Change: Advancing Education, Income and Health Through Collective Impact*. As well as his 2013 *Goals for the Common Good - The United Way Challenge for America*. For a pdf, visit www.RealizingDreams.us/Resources/United-Way.

A Popcorn Machine

I also believe America needs Einsteinian thinking to solve our entrenched social issues so that we can keep our great American dream alive. After giving Chuck Salkala, the Executive Director of the National Auto Body Council, a few creative ideas he called me a "popcorn

machine". As background I met Chuck in June 2012 at the SkillsUSA national conference. We engaged in meaningful and heartfelt conversations and he shared that the National Auto Body Council wanted to continuously improve the way they were communicating parts to mechanics - within seconds a few creative ideas just popped into my head.

I told Chuck my inspiration came from the quotes on the cards in the game edition and now they are in the *7 Steps for EMPOWERING YOUTH*. Based on this and other experiences, I believe it will inspire a few creative ideas to solve other problems for you as well.

So for the first time in a published book, I offer a few of my other 20 or so creative ideas that just "popped" into my head. These are what I call my Einstein inspired and infused teaching formulas. Some coaches refer to this as "brain food". These formulas help us develop our grit and a growth mindset that fosters resilience for exponential achievement in school, work, life, health and play. I also refer to these

as self-efficacy formulas that develop Life Skill Assets™ for success in our ever changing 21st century. For more, visit www.RealizingDreams.us.

My hope is that these formulas, woven into the activities of this LifeBook™, will further empower all of us to collaborate for community change for collective impact. I truly believe that to transform lives we must synchronize the energy and experience of our generations so that youth learn the easy way and not make the same mistakes as adults.

I also believe one of our purposes in life is to inspire potential in ourselves so that we can inspire potential in others and that this is what makes it easier and empowers our future generations to realize their dreams and achieve greater life outcomes. So, if you too believe that we need to engage, equip and

empower our youth with the skills for self-efficacy so that they self-actualize and reach their full potential, please accept this invitation to join in the collective impact initiatives including **Mission: USA 2020**. United, we can solve our education, income and health challenges.

MISSION: USA 2020

By 2020, engage, equip and empower 90% of America's 42+ million youth with self-awareness, GRIT and a growth mindset to reach their full potential.

I proudly join in!

Name: _____

Signature: _____

School: _____

Grade _____ or Year in College _____ Date: _____

"A small body of determined spirits fired by
an unquenchable faith in their mission can
alter the course of history."

~ Gandhi

A Closing Note

Thank you for reading *7 Steps for EMPOWERING YOUTH.* With your GRIT and growth mindset, I hope you are now more self-aware, self-propelled and on your way to self-actualization.

If you have not already completed Step 7, I invite you to join **MISSION: USA 2020** on the previous page. If you have, congratulations!

In closing, Give inspiration... Get inspired™. As this GivaGeta™ saying goes, if I inspired you, and you have a few moments to share, it would great to hear from you as I love getting inspired too.

Thank you for letting me be a part of realizing the dreams in your life.

Gratefully yours,

James Louis Cantoni, Sr

Share your journey with us at www.RealizingDreams.us and on social media at:

 @MissionUSA2020   RealizingDreams.us

Acknowledgements

To all the friends, students, families, teachers, counselors and community leaders who participated in the pilots of the 7 Steps for EMPOWERING YOUTH the self-discovery Lifebook and The Student Dream Kit over the last 24+ months. YOU all helped me realize one of my dreams in life, a heartfelt thank you!

First, a special thanks to Cara Campo and her dad, Tony Rescigno, who both believed in me, as well as the New Haven Public School students in the pilot– William Jr., Jaila, Terence and Talani. Thank you to Shirley Ma and her children, Spencer and Brady and their friends. To the Rondinelli Family: Giovanni, Yola, Lisa- a future pharmacist, Kara- you will do great things with robotics; thanks for being the first family to sign up for the pilot. Thank you to my nephew and niece, Sam Ferreira and Veronica Johnson, who want to be the best they can be. Thank you to Veronica's cousins: Callie, you will someday design and model your own clothing line; Zachary, I hope I get invited to visit you in Los Angeles when you become a pro-gamer! To Dr. Carol Merlone, Michael Maziarz, Josh Reese and McKinley Albert, thank you for believing in me and giving me a chance. To Kim Pita and Manny and Diana Rivera, thank you for your big hearts and helping me through the years. Dr. Joni Samples, thank you for believing in and inspiring me further!

Thank you Dan Hecker and Michael Turovac. Thank you Shan Bhagat– save me a room in one of your hotels. Thank you Susan Dunn, CEO of our local United Way, for believing in me too. To the Girl Scout leader and grandmother, a heartfelt thank you for the inspiration of Teamwork and FamilyPlay the game which led to *7 Steps for EMPOWERING YOUTH*. To Dr. Jim Cain, a remarkable author of many active learning books, and renowned world trainer, thank you for the opportunity to collaborate on the Teamwork and Teamplay edition; it truly is a remarkable team building tool.

To Seth Godin, author of many thought leading books including *Purple Cow* and *The Lynchpin*, thanks for inspiring me to strive to be remarkable, produce interactions that people care deeply about and lastly, to "ship". To Jim Collins, author of *Good to Great* and *Great by Choice*, you are the Peter Drucker of our day and, like the many greats before us, your research resonates with us and inspires us to be the

best we can be. To Christine Cashin, dynamic speaker, humorista and author of *The Good Stuff*, your smile and bubbly way helps show the lighter side of life. I'm smiling back at you!

A big shout out of thanks to Lynn Mika, who shared many hours getting my Adobe InDesign experience up and focused. I hope I can help you with your book about GOO. Kudos to my wonderful nephew, Remie Ferreira, my sons, Jimmy, Jr. and Nathan and to my beautiful wife, Jackie, who helped create the game and books. Thanks to upcoming "Level 5 Leader" Robby Kasper who at 16 years old, inspired the name "My Big Answer" and was instrumental with the edits in this lifebook.

Gratitude to Jennifer and Michael Loscialpo, two remarkable people who "dare to inspire" us all. Thanks to their children, who gave up part of a wonderful snowy day to help with the games and activities. Special appreciation goes to Kristi Allen, a journalism major, for her remarkable writing insight. A "GIANT THANK YOU" to Claudia Danna whose edits led me down to the finish line! For the fourth edition, thank you to Noel Pardo, Troy Bennett, Tracy Verrastro, Shane O'Brien, Amanda Reese, Mike Cotela, Peggy Palomba, Keith Garbart, Nancy Hoyt, Mary Crombie, Doug Fairbanks, Aksana Solter, Rosetta Salmon, and the many youth and adults who believed in me and helped with the name change and new cover design for *7 Steps for EMPOWERING YOUTH*. Thank you. You all helped me realize this dream as a team!

Lastly, thank you again to all the youth and adults who participated in the workshops, especially Aiden, a very inspiring teen who, like all of you, are helping make the world a better place for all.

Notes:

_____

_____

_____

_____

_____

_____

_____

_____

_____

_____

_____

_____

Thank you for reading

7 Steps for EMPOWERING YOUTH!

If you would like to obtain additional copies of *7 Steps for EMPOWERING YOUTH* or to invite Jim Cantoni to facilitate your groups at staff training, positive youth development with GRIT and Growth Mindset workshops or at your school-family-community partnerships to improve youth outcomes, please contact Jim at:

Realizing Dreams
T: 860.657.0770
www.RealizingDreams.us

Bookmark

What Education Experts are Saying:

In his *7 Steps for EMPOWERING YOUTH: Developing GRIT and a Growth Mindset*, Jim Cantoni gives you practical and easy ways to engage in some of the most important self-discovery conversations you'll ever have— those with your children that create learning.

All of us who do work around Family Engagement talk about collaboration and respect. In order for schools, families and communities to create partnerships in which the children are the recipients of adult decisions, we need to develop a level of trust and cooperation. Jim's materials, this one, and others he has developed focus our attention, the attention of the family, on character and mindful self-awareness. As a Mom of four children as well as a consummate educator, I want character AND learning.

7 Steps for EMPOWERING YOUTH is a must have for parents and school folks alike.

– Dr. Joni Samples
Chief Academic Officer of Family Friendly Schools